Embark on a vibrant and creative journey with our coloring book specially designed to inspire children's imagination.

Each page is a unique adventure, inviting children to unleash their creativity as they fill every blank space with the most cheerful colors they can imagine.

From magical animals to fantastic landscapes, this book provides a coloring experience that goes beyond the pages, encouraging artistic expression and motor skill development.

This charming book is perfect for curious children who love to create and explore a world full of colors and fantasy.

Let the fun begin as little ones dive into this magical and creative coloring adventure!

Color Test

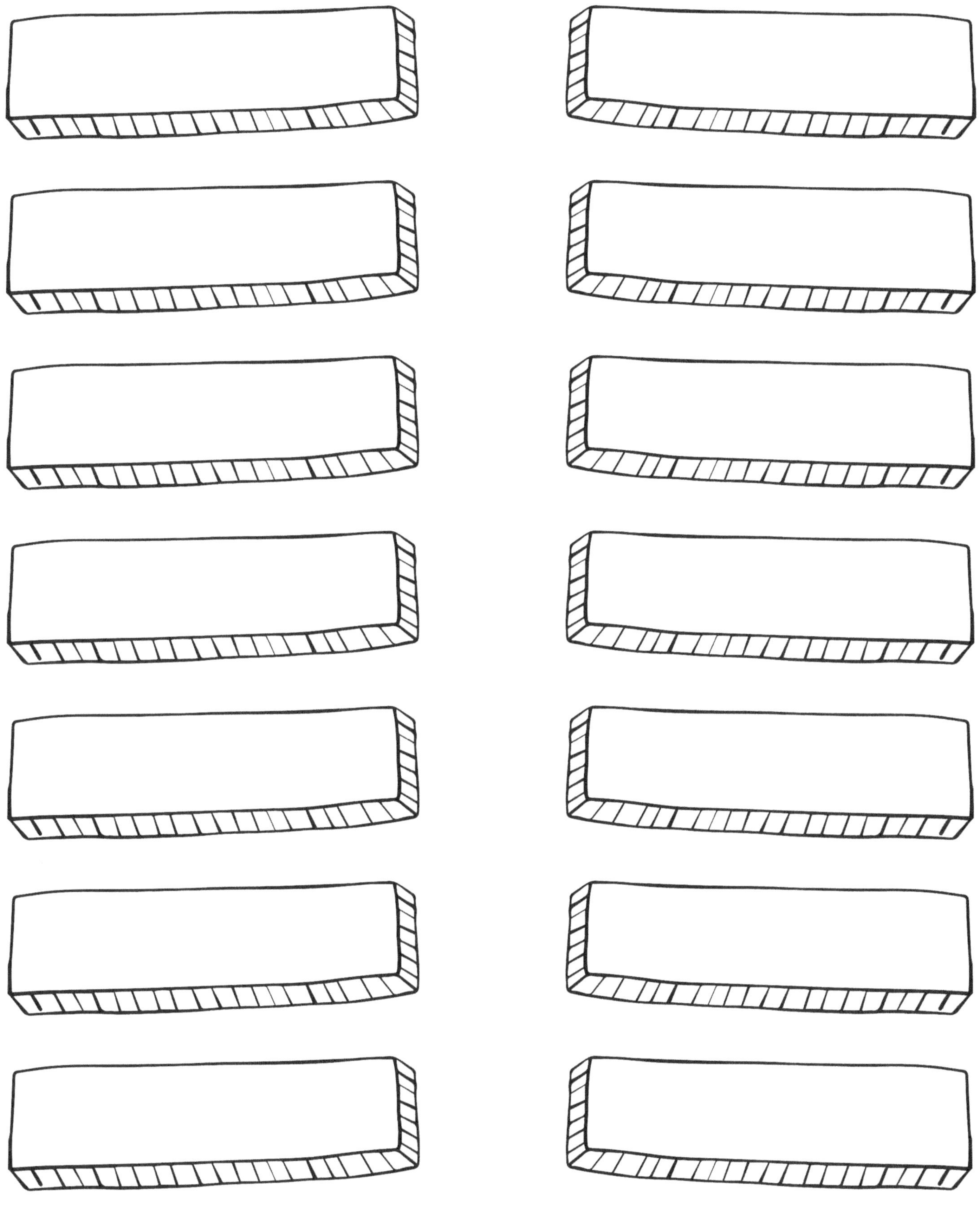

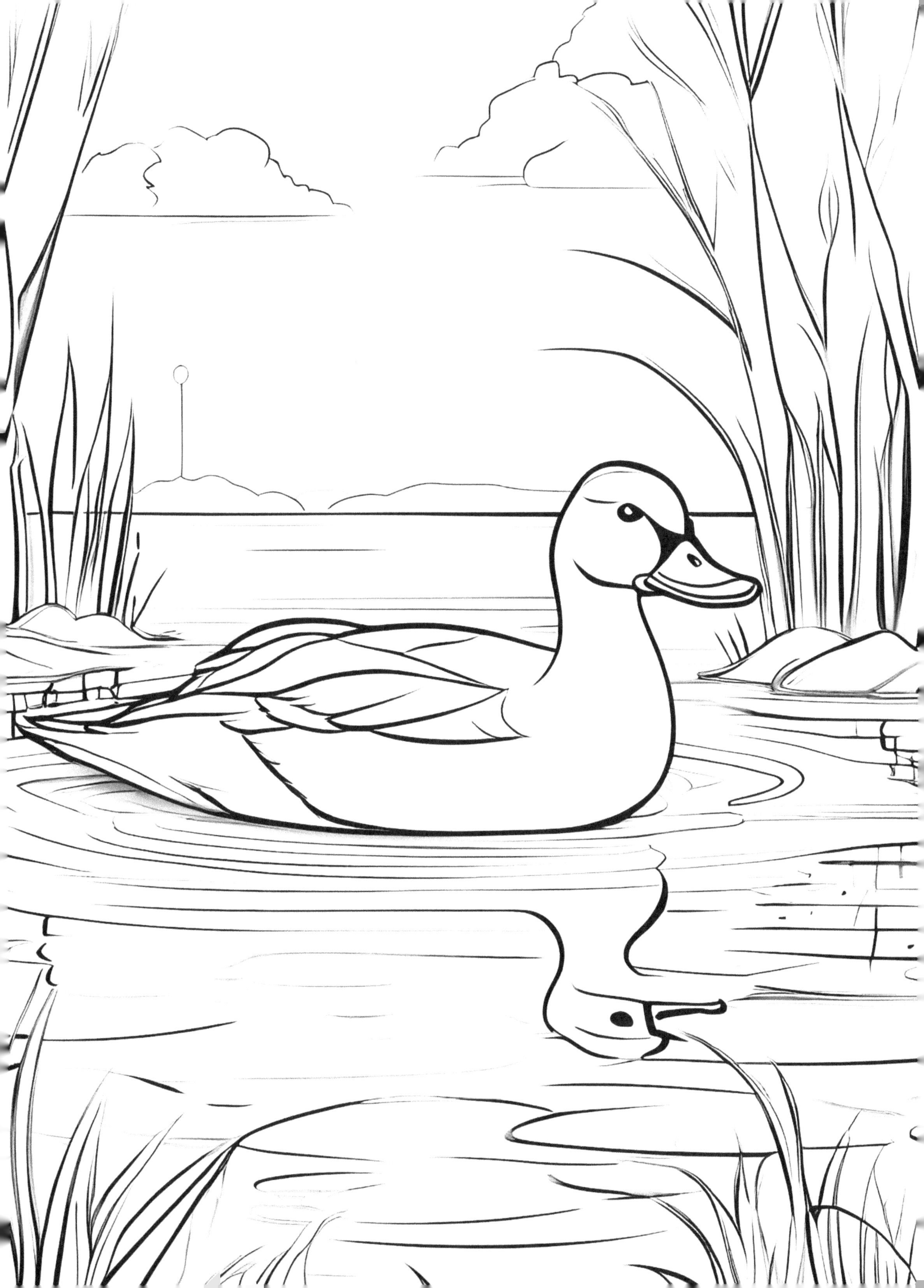

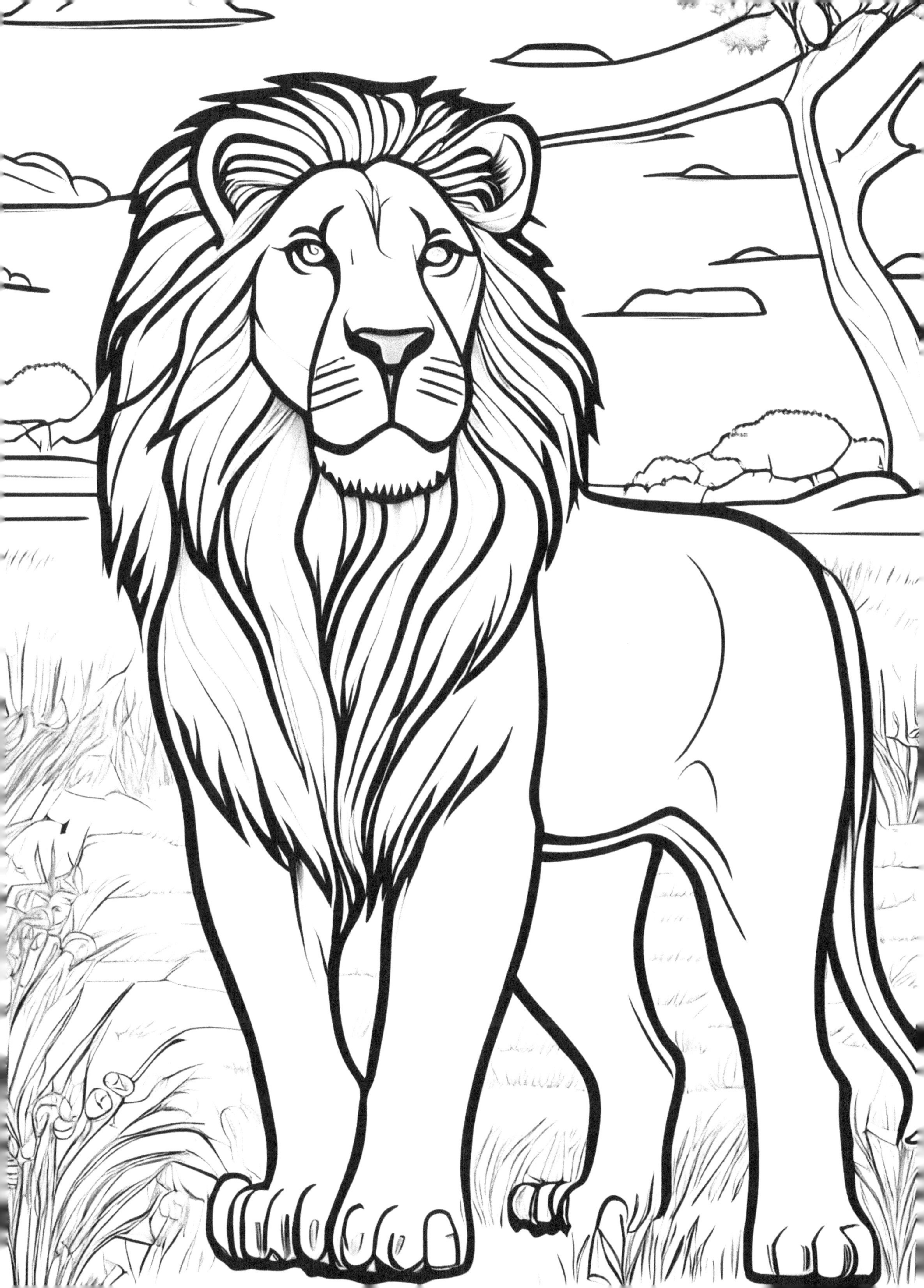

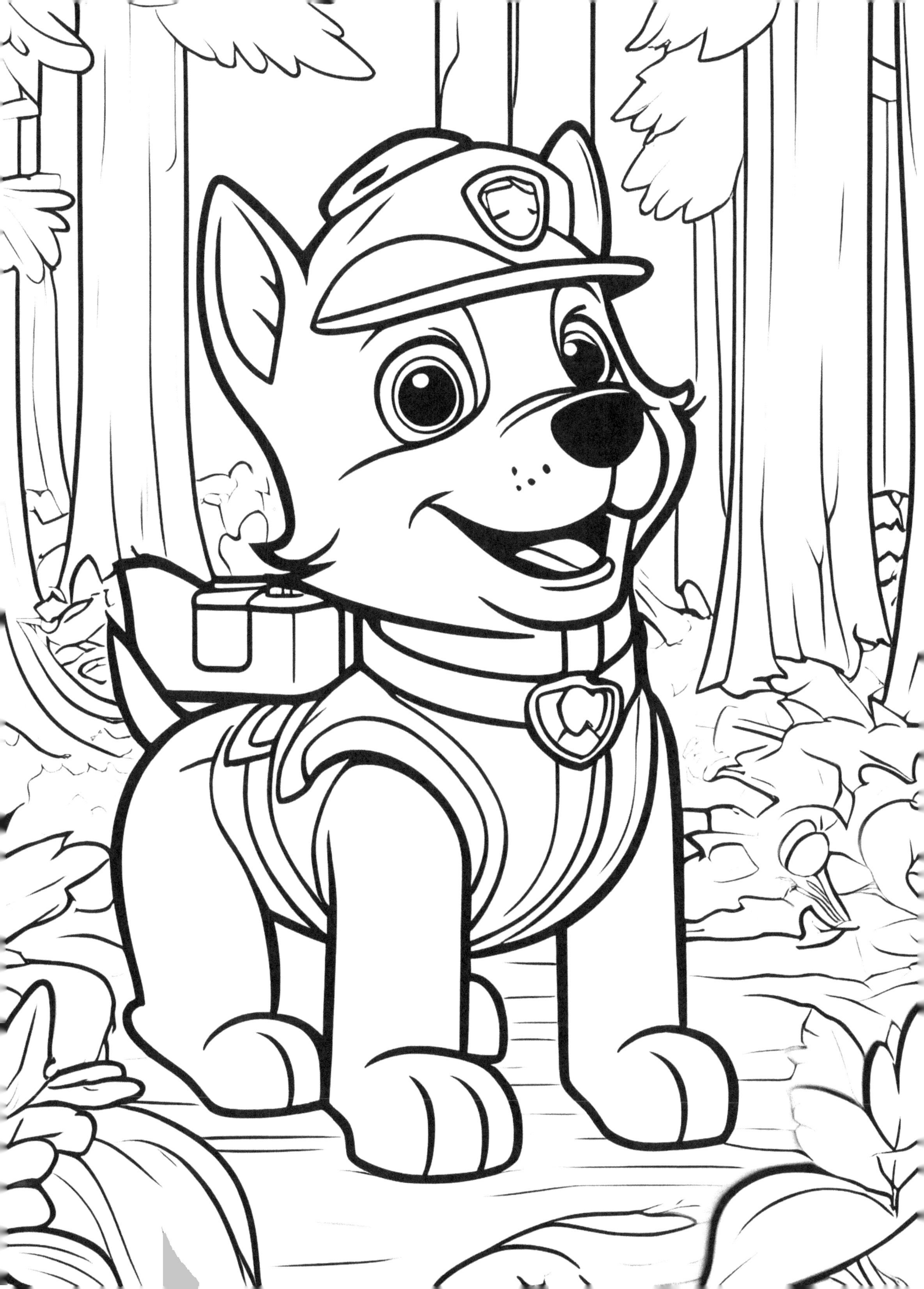

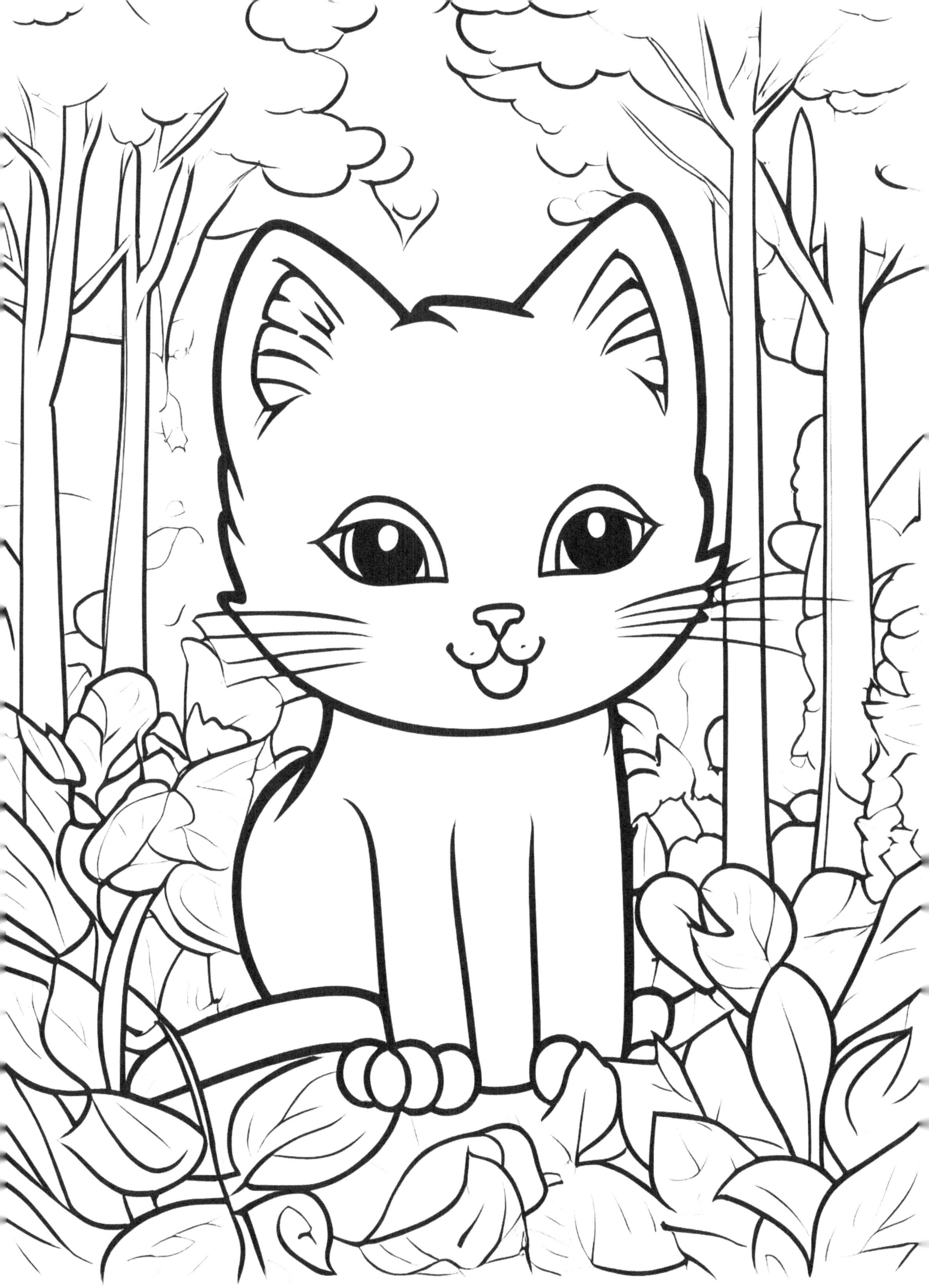

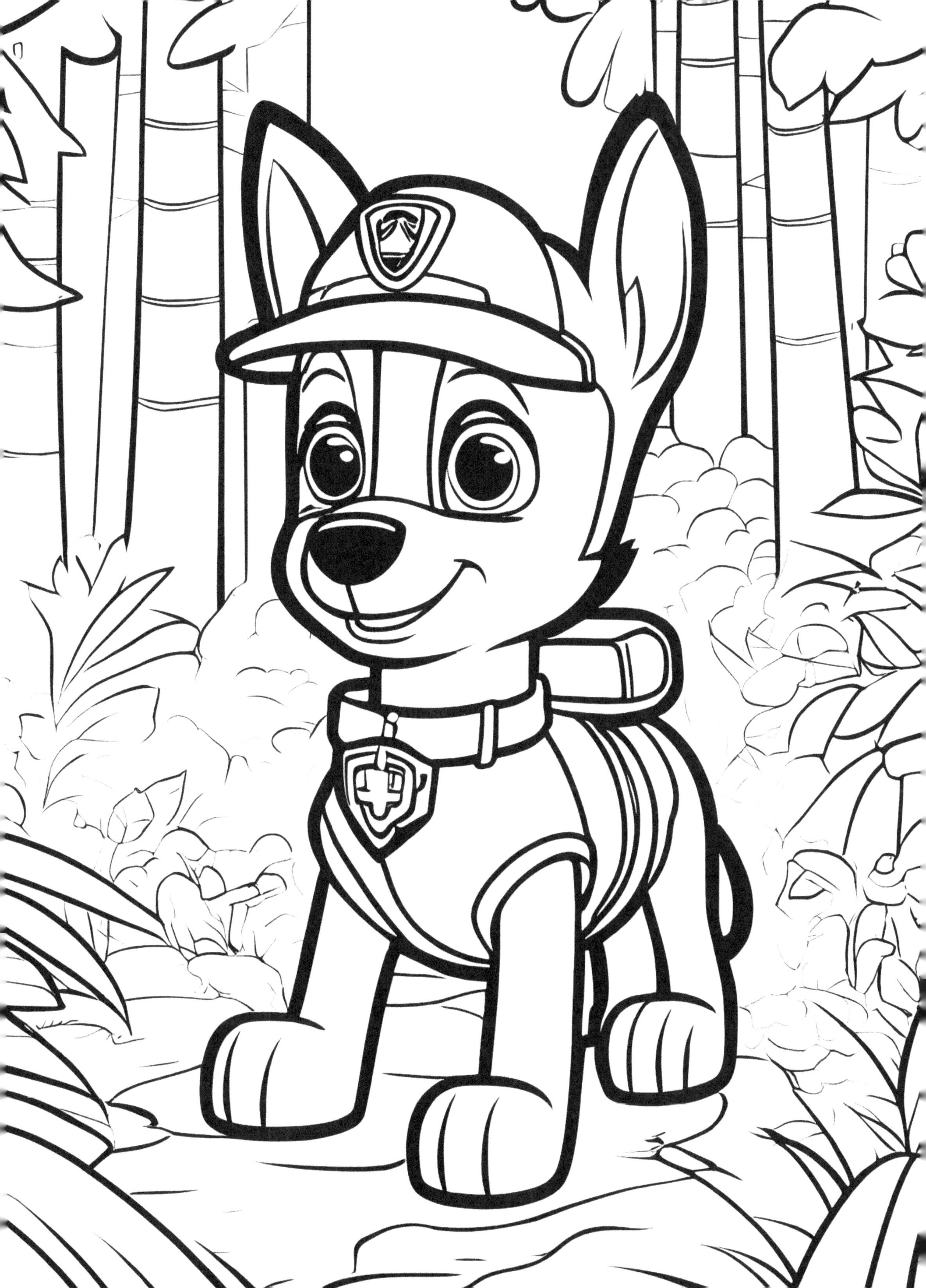

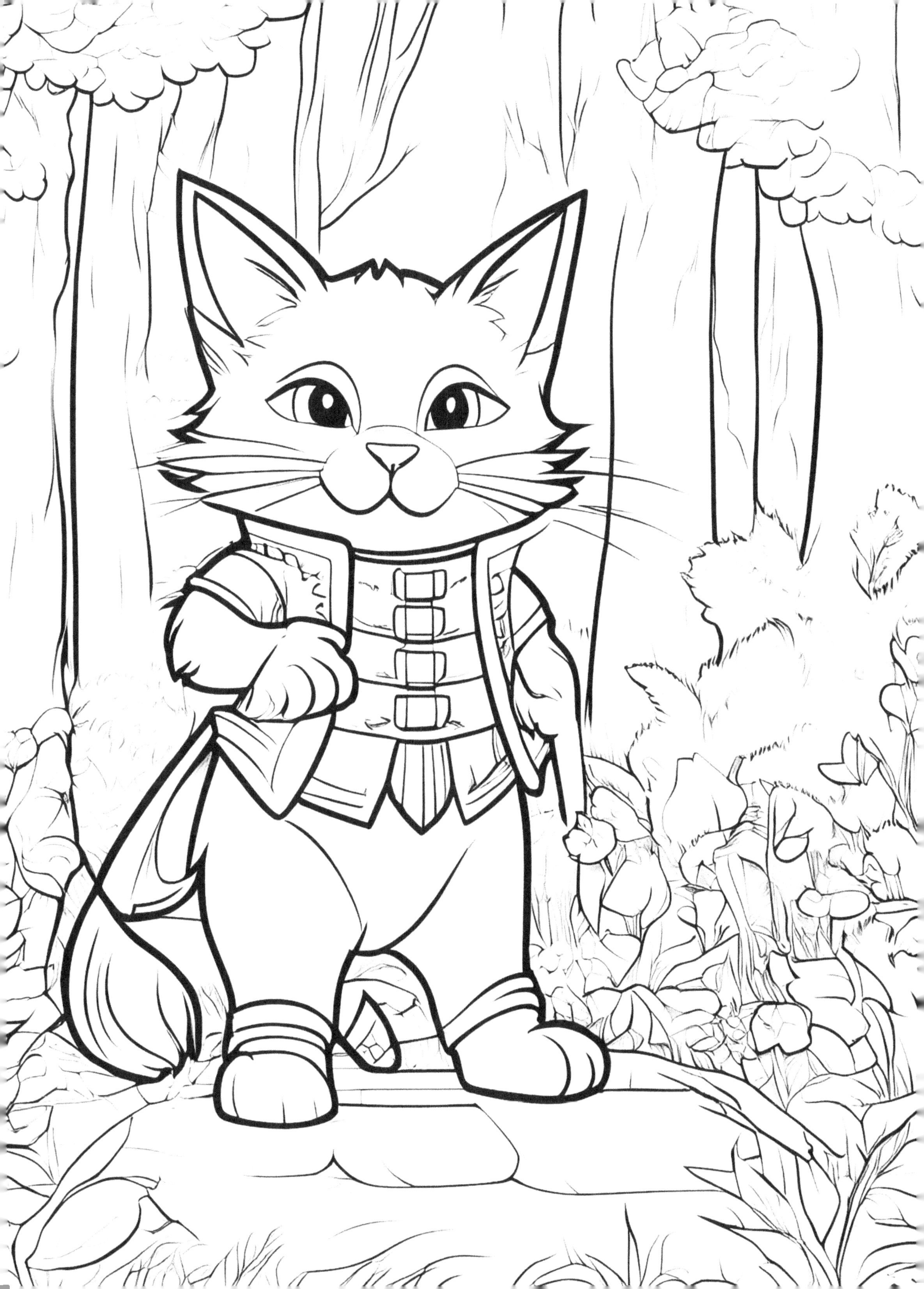

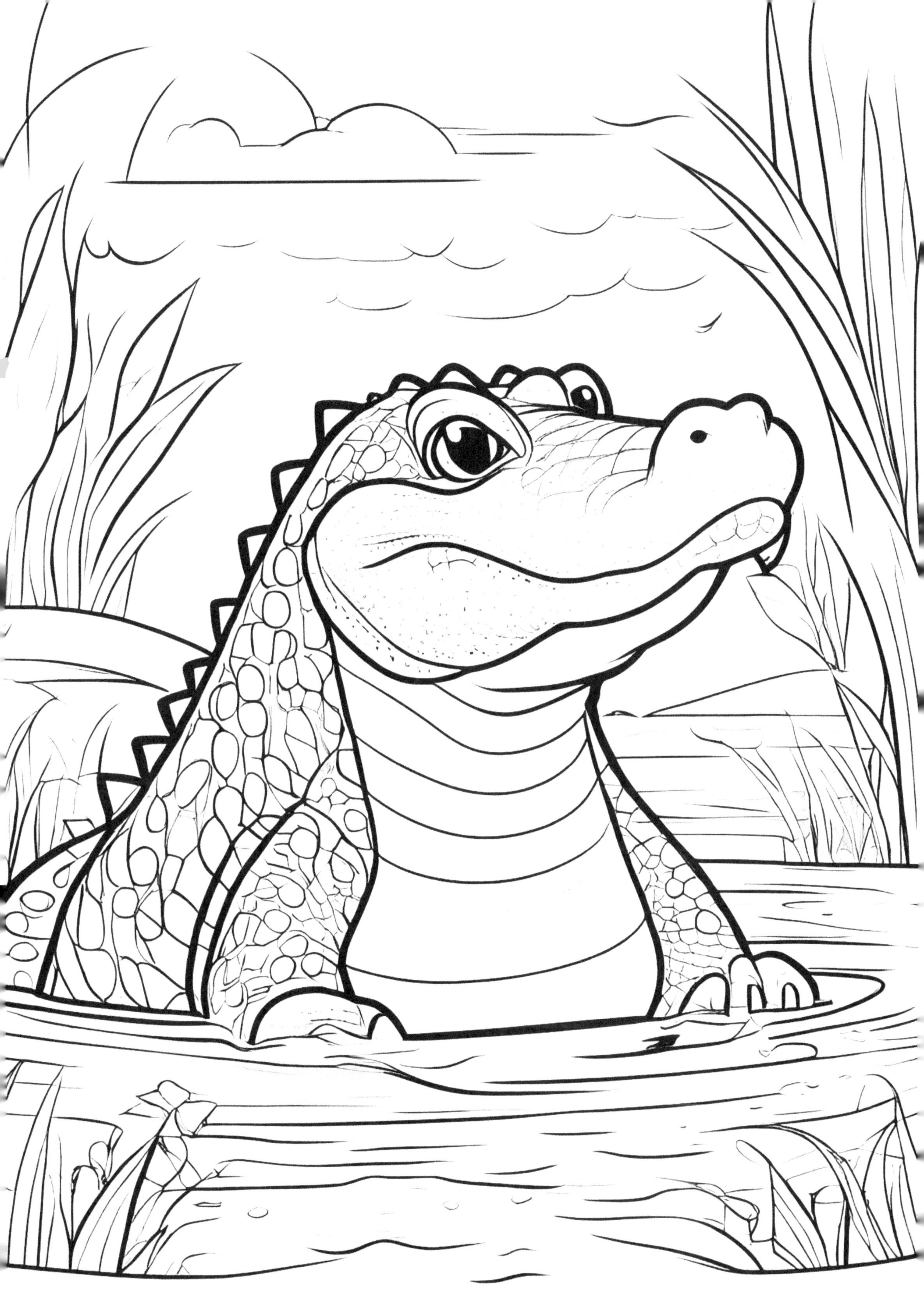

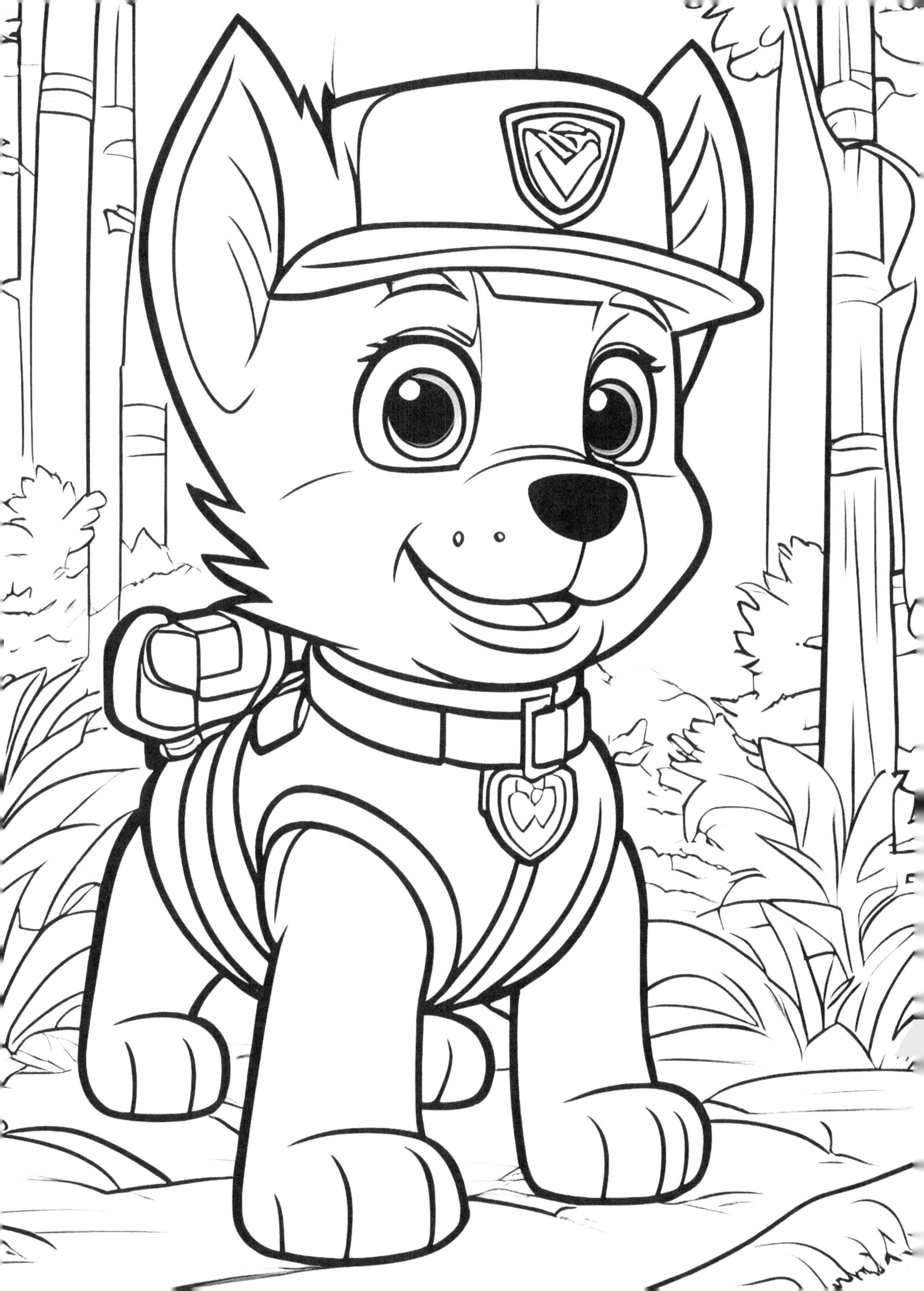

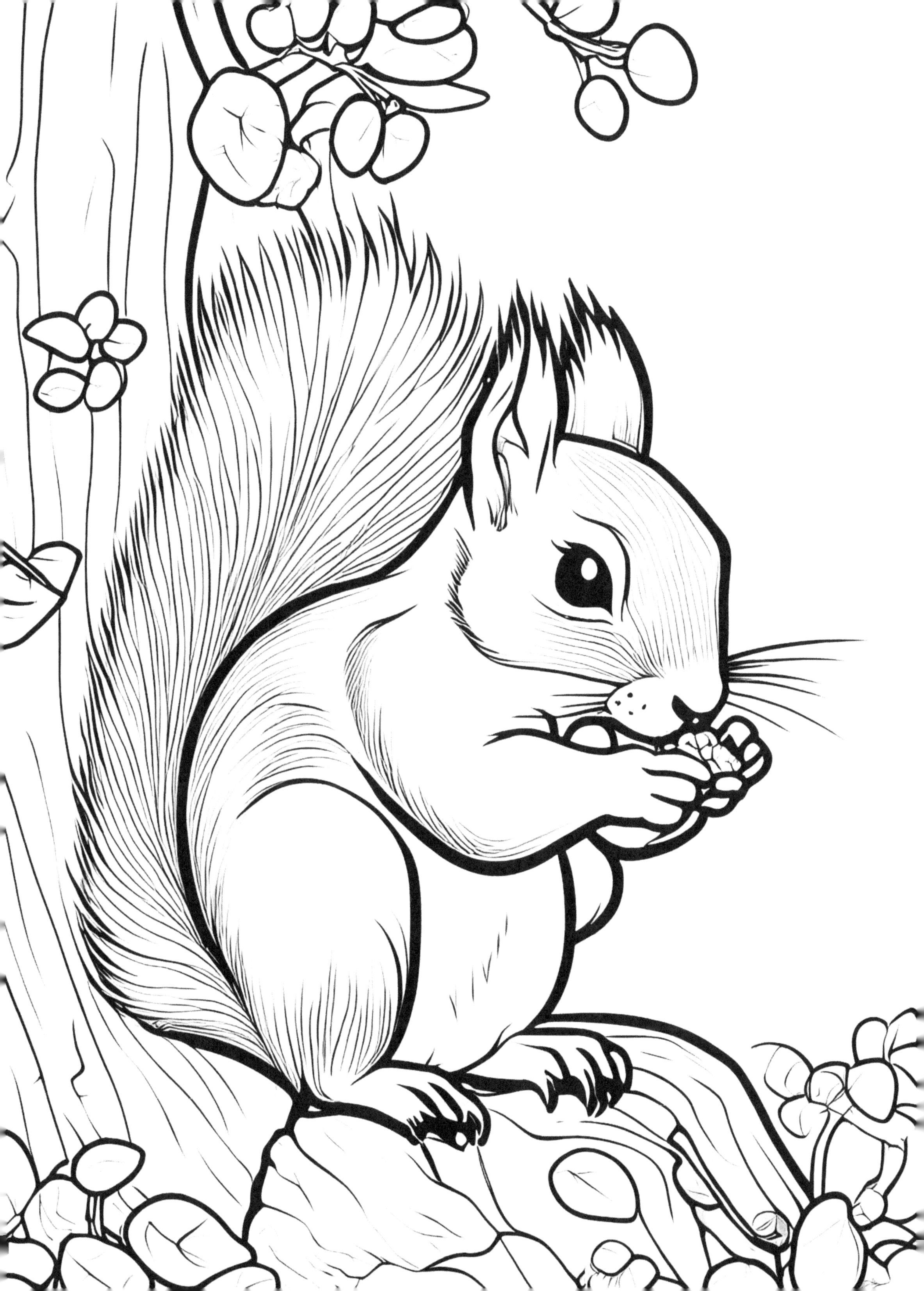

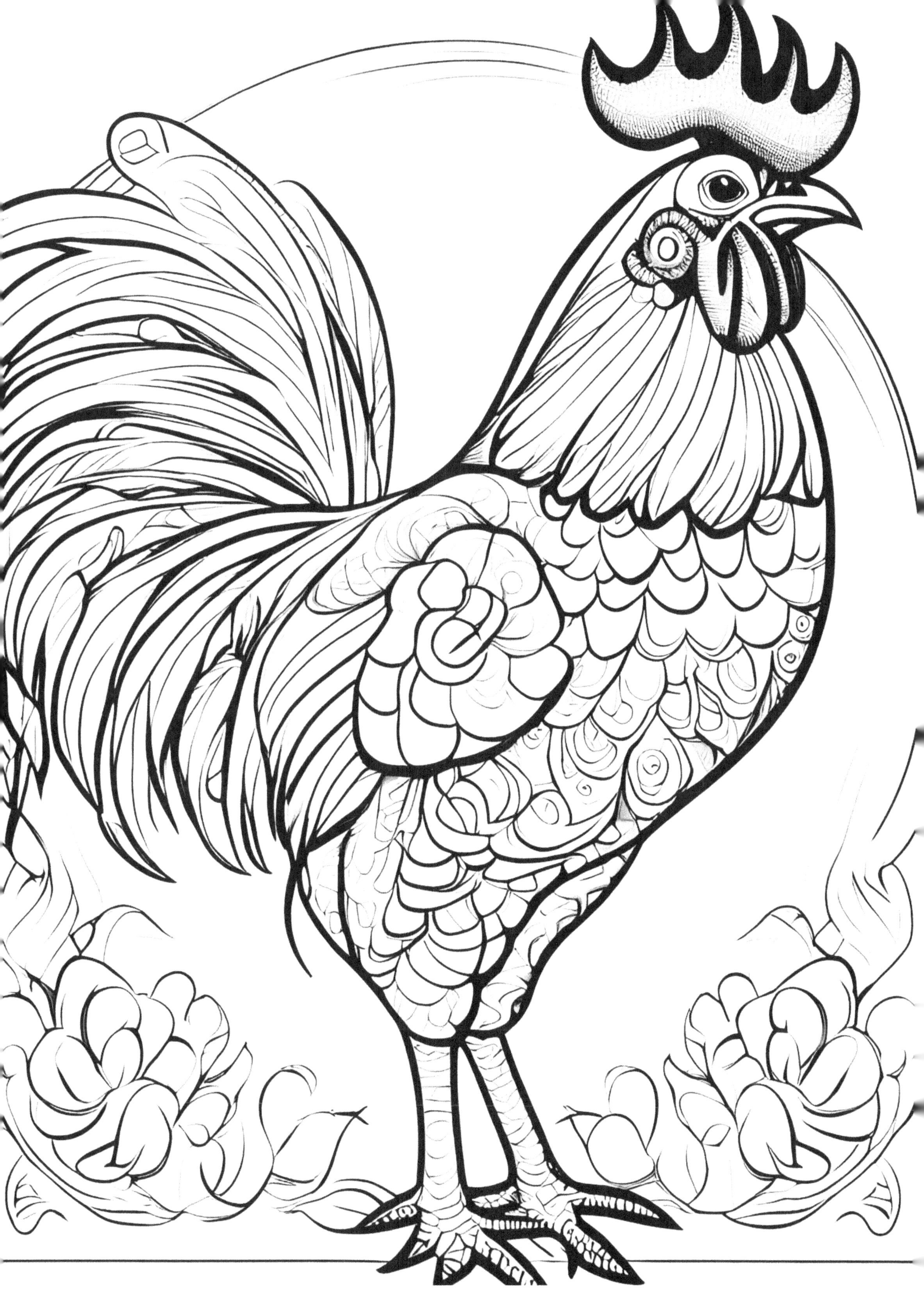

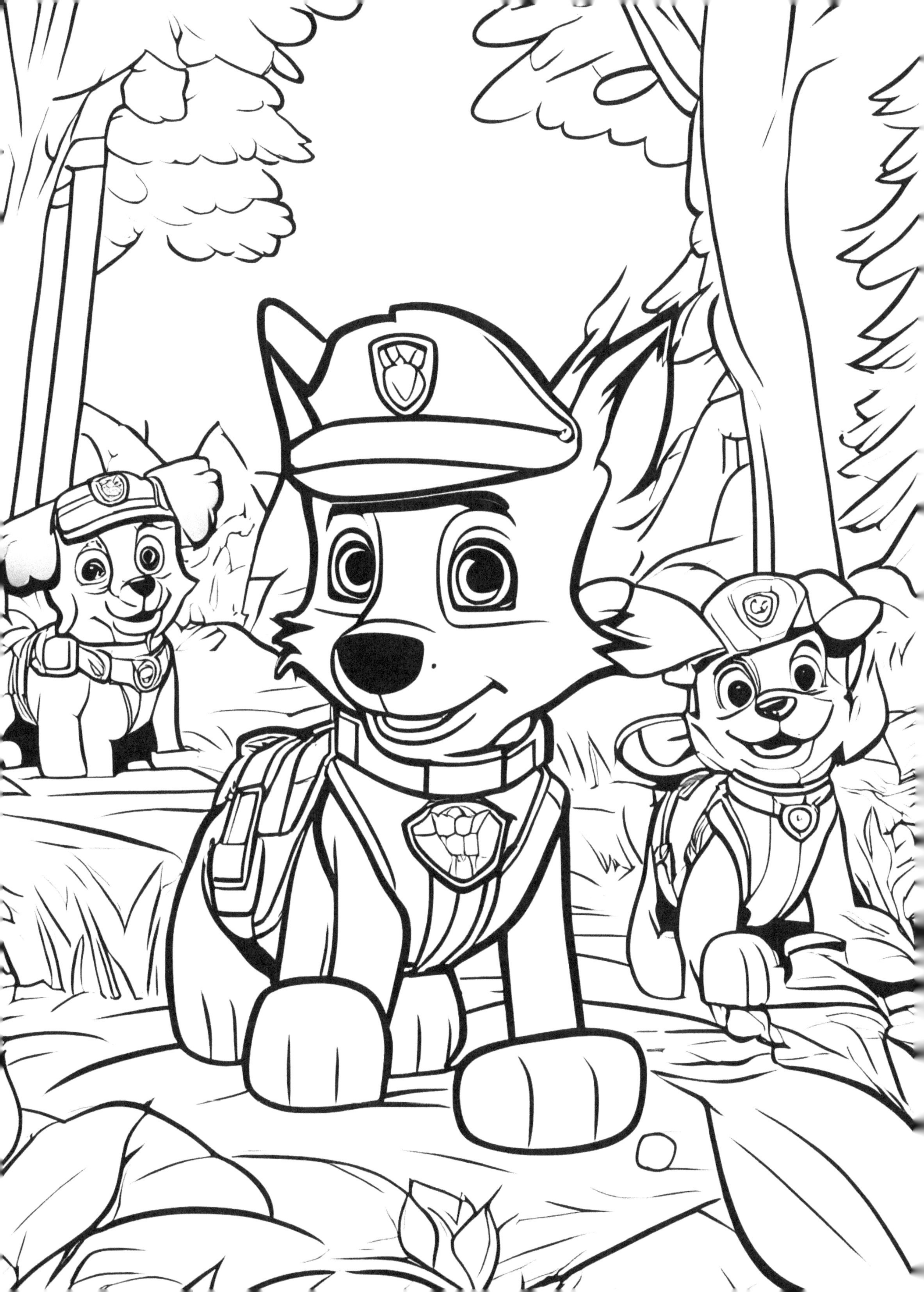

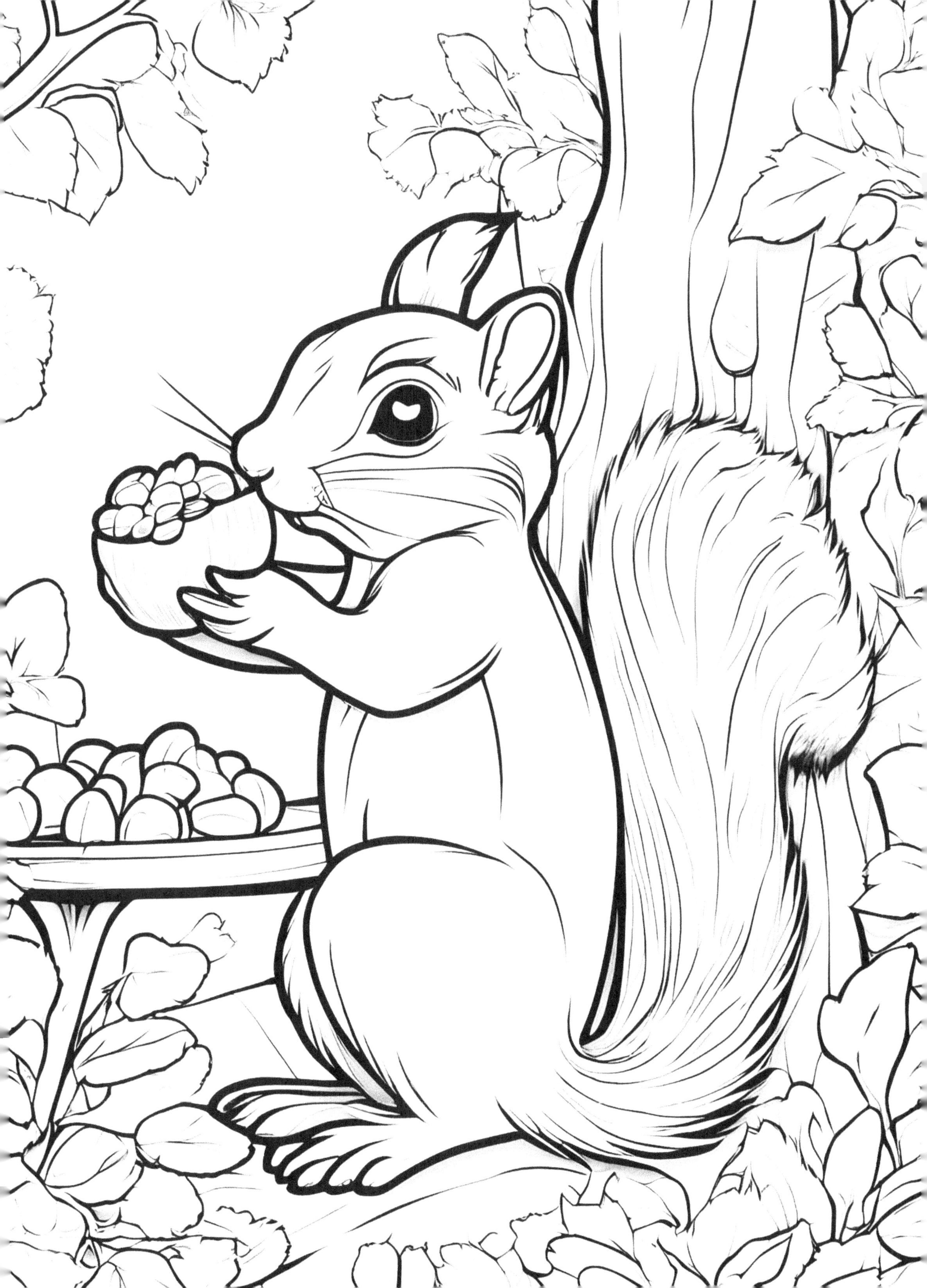

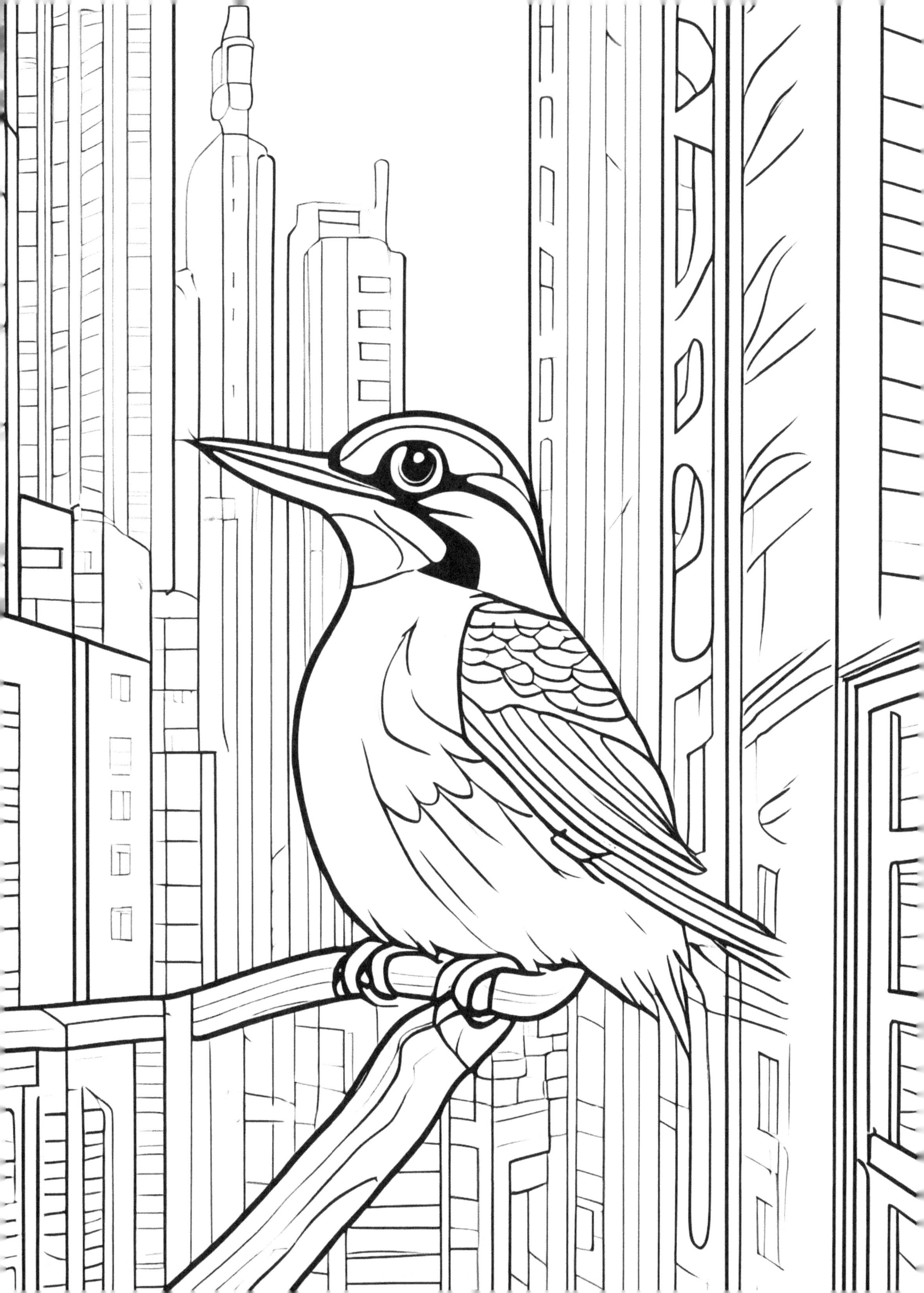

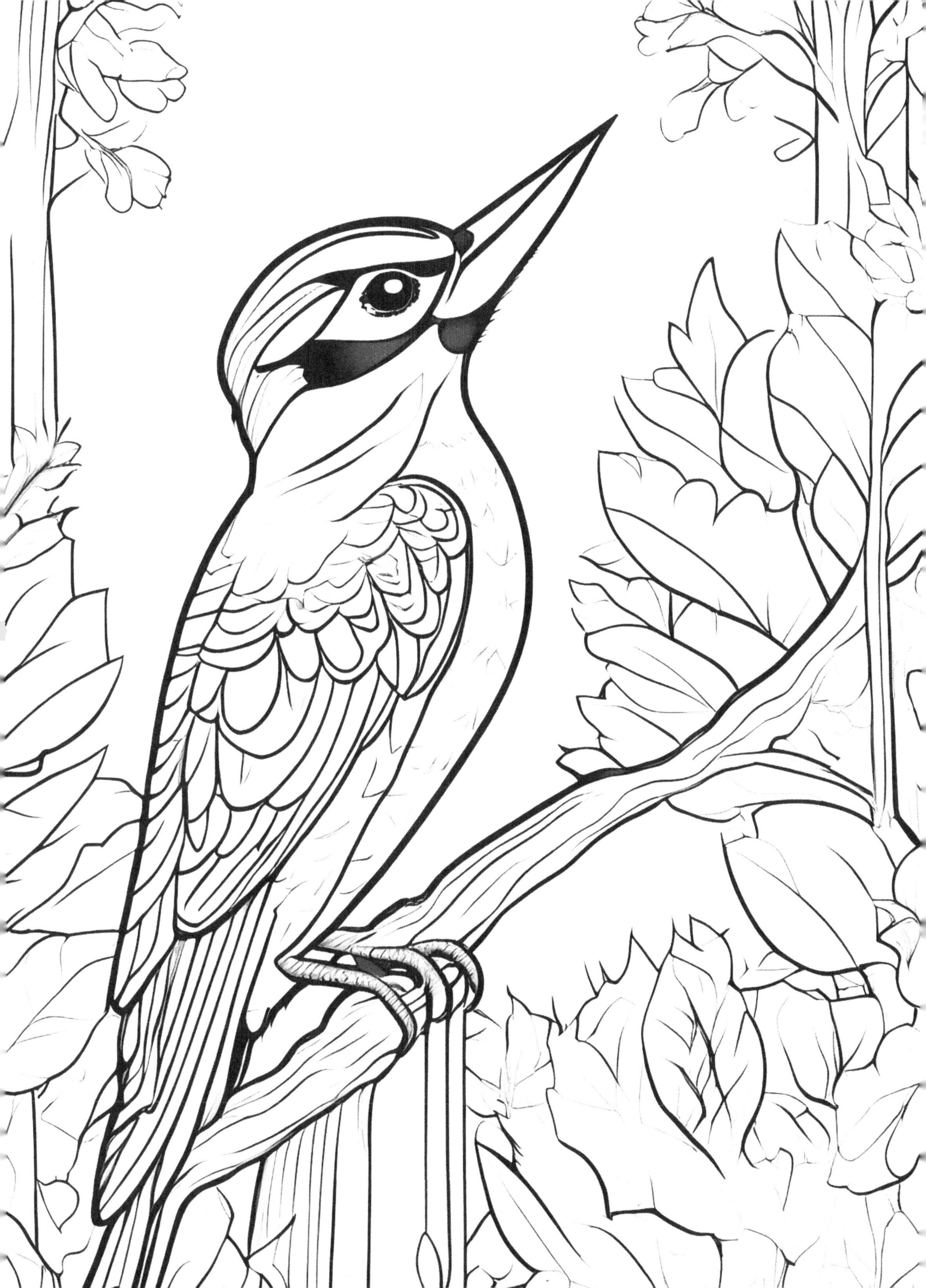

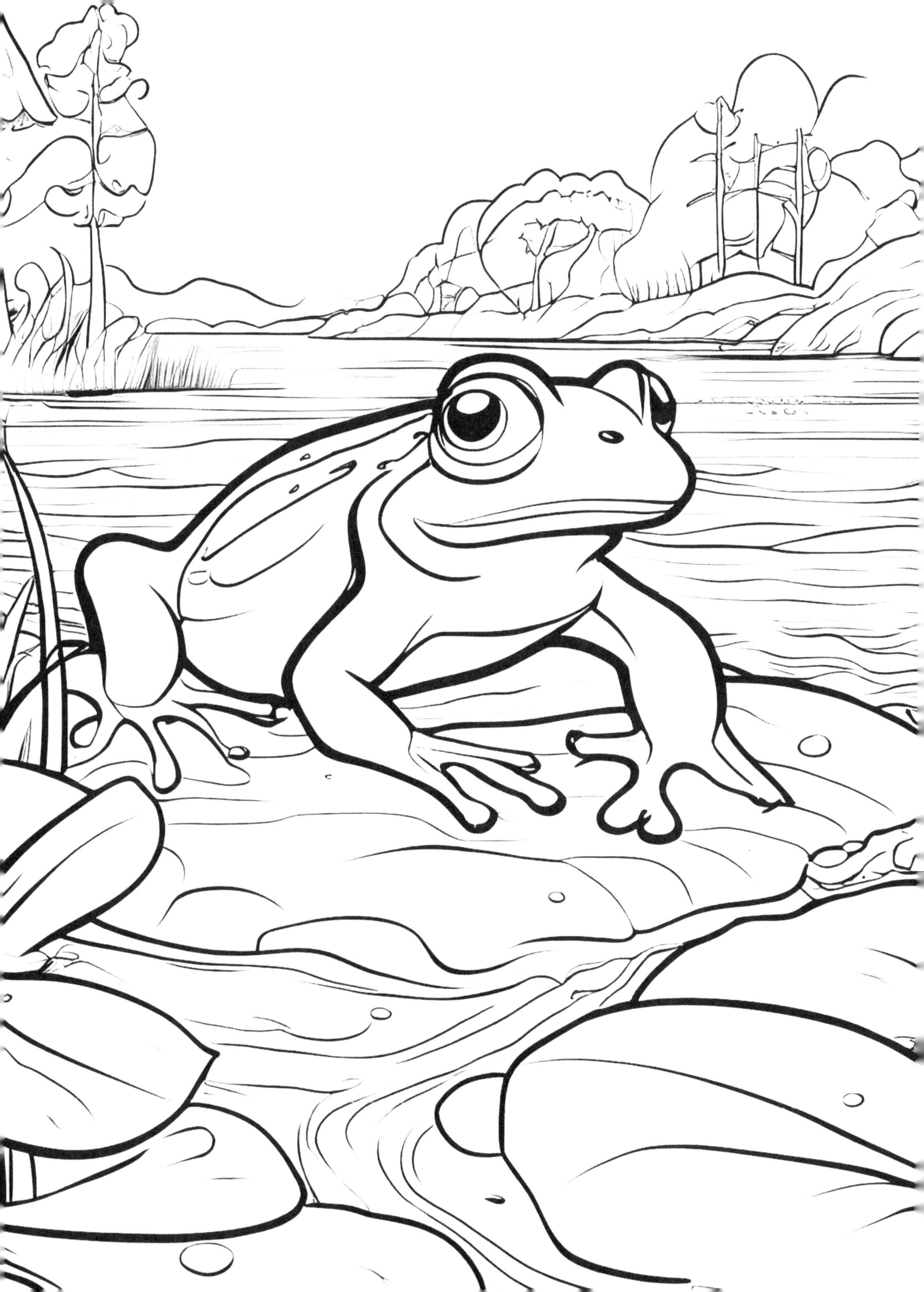

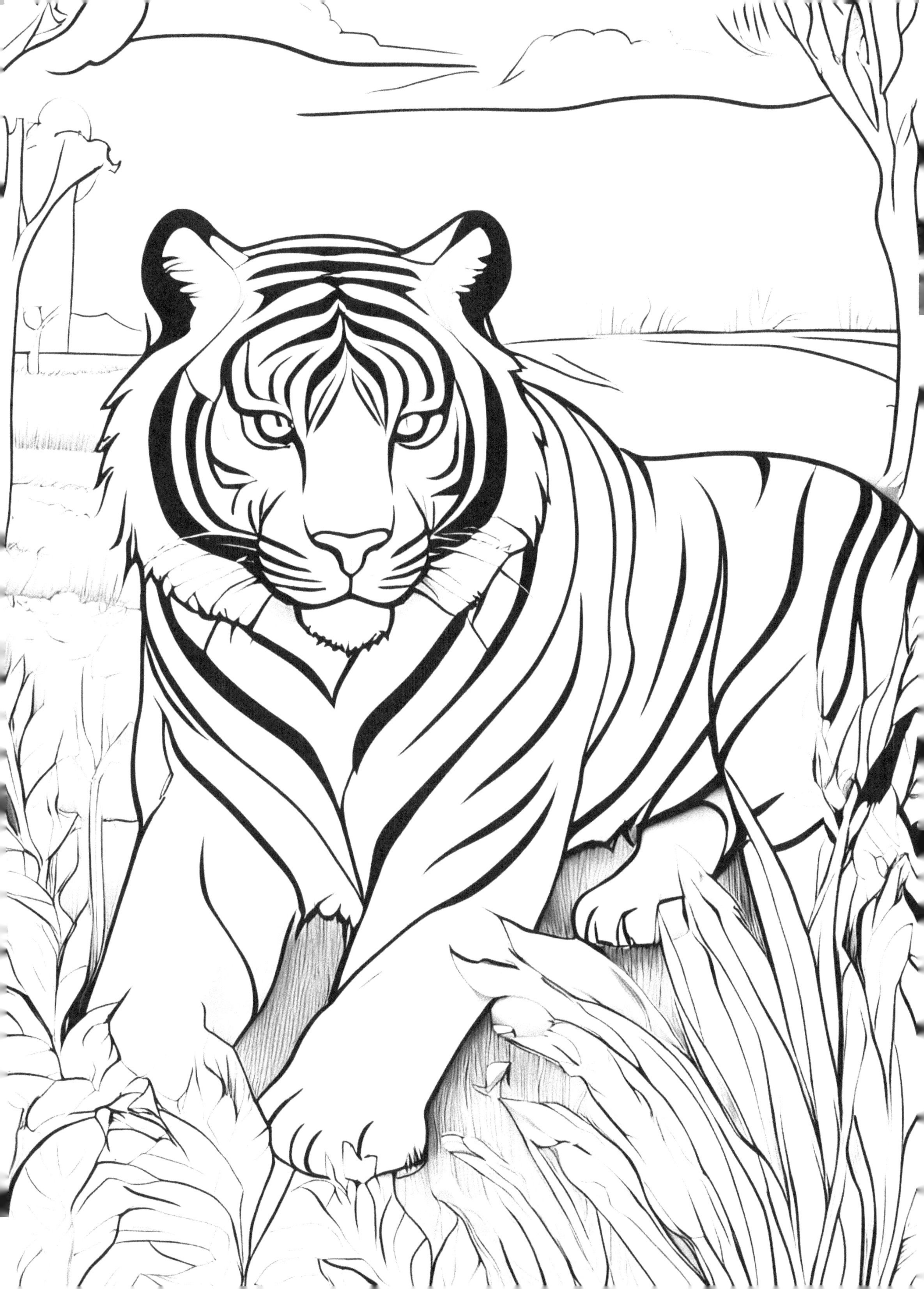

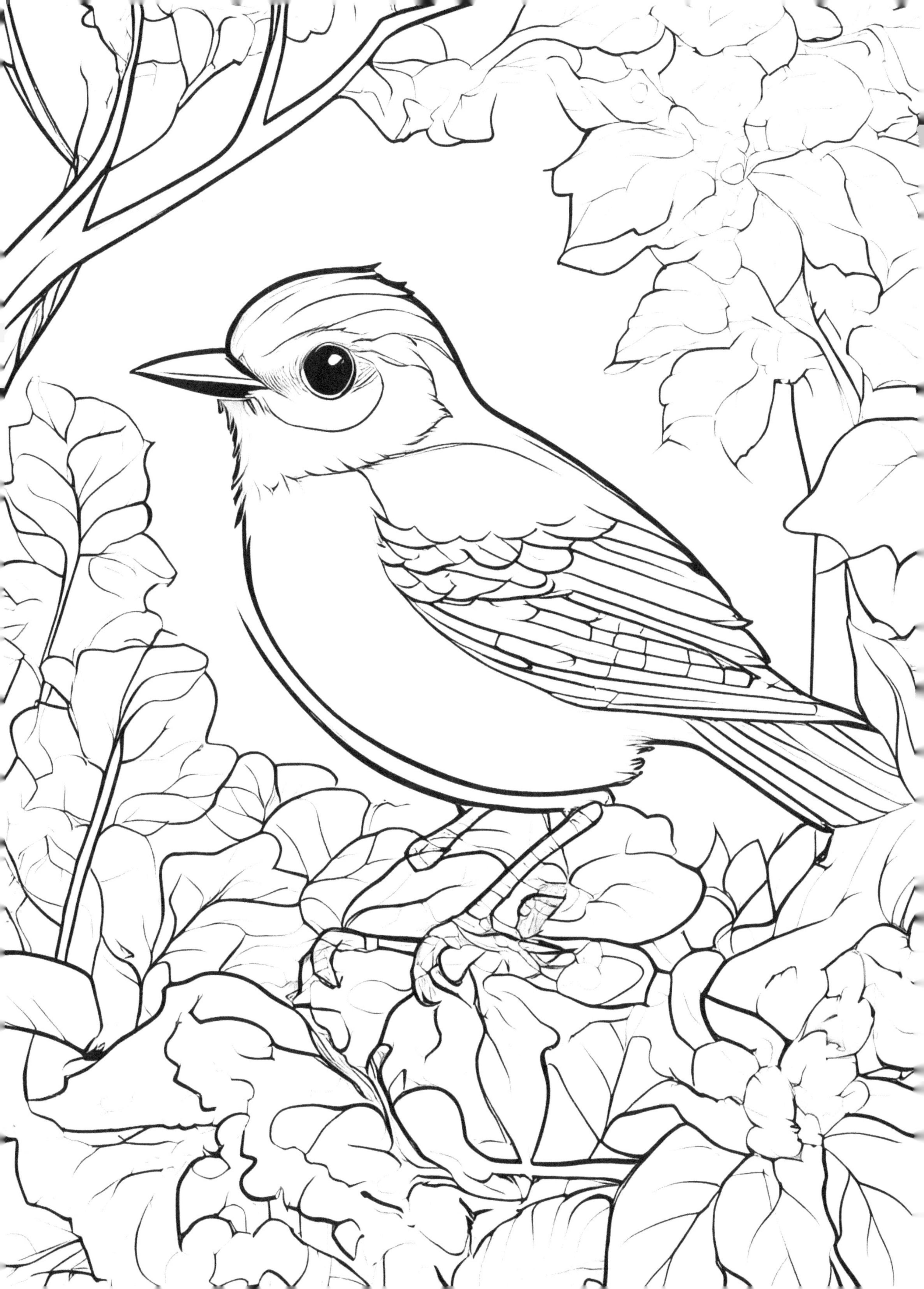

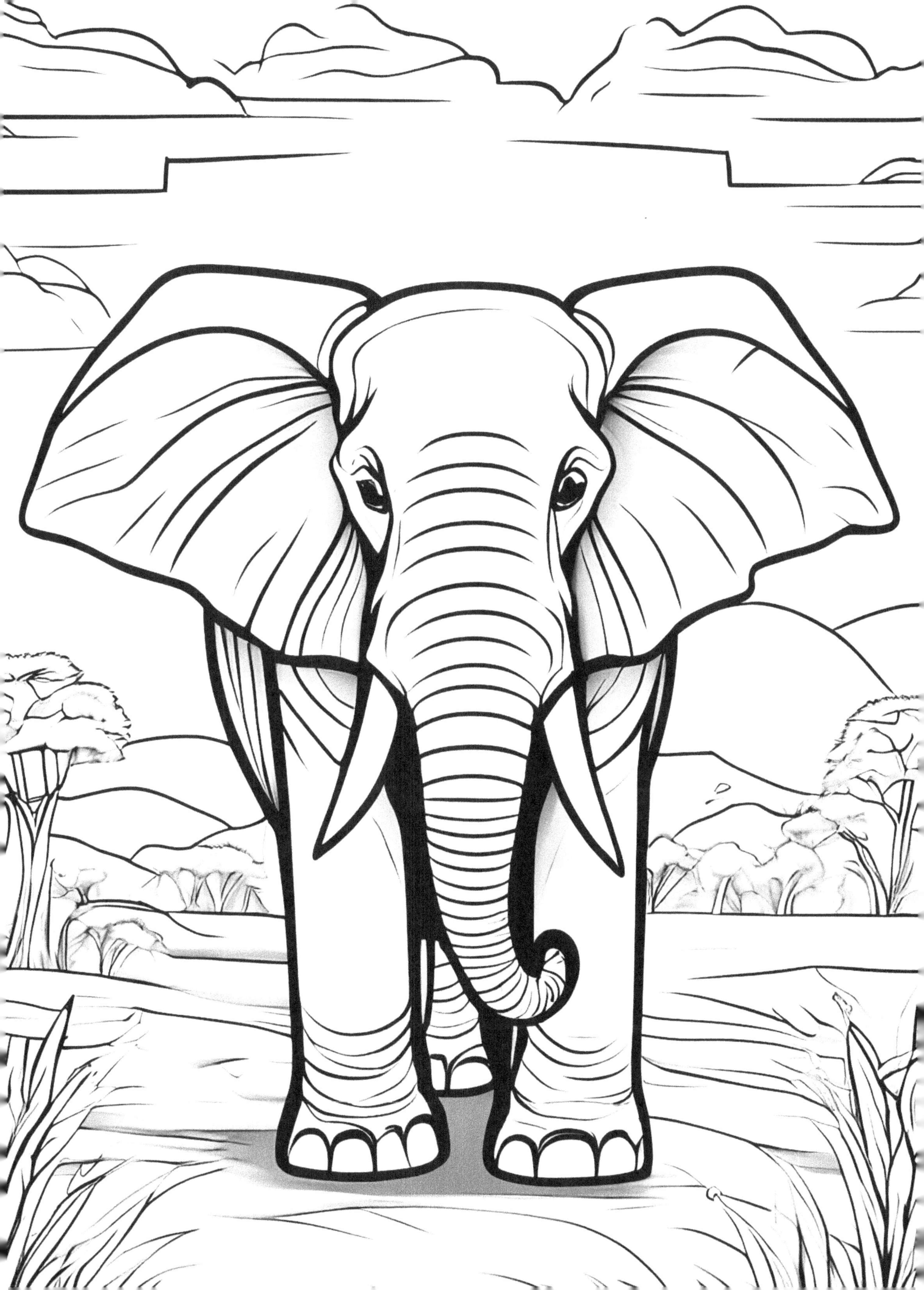

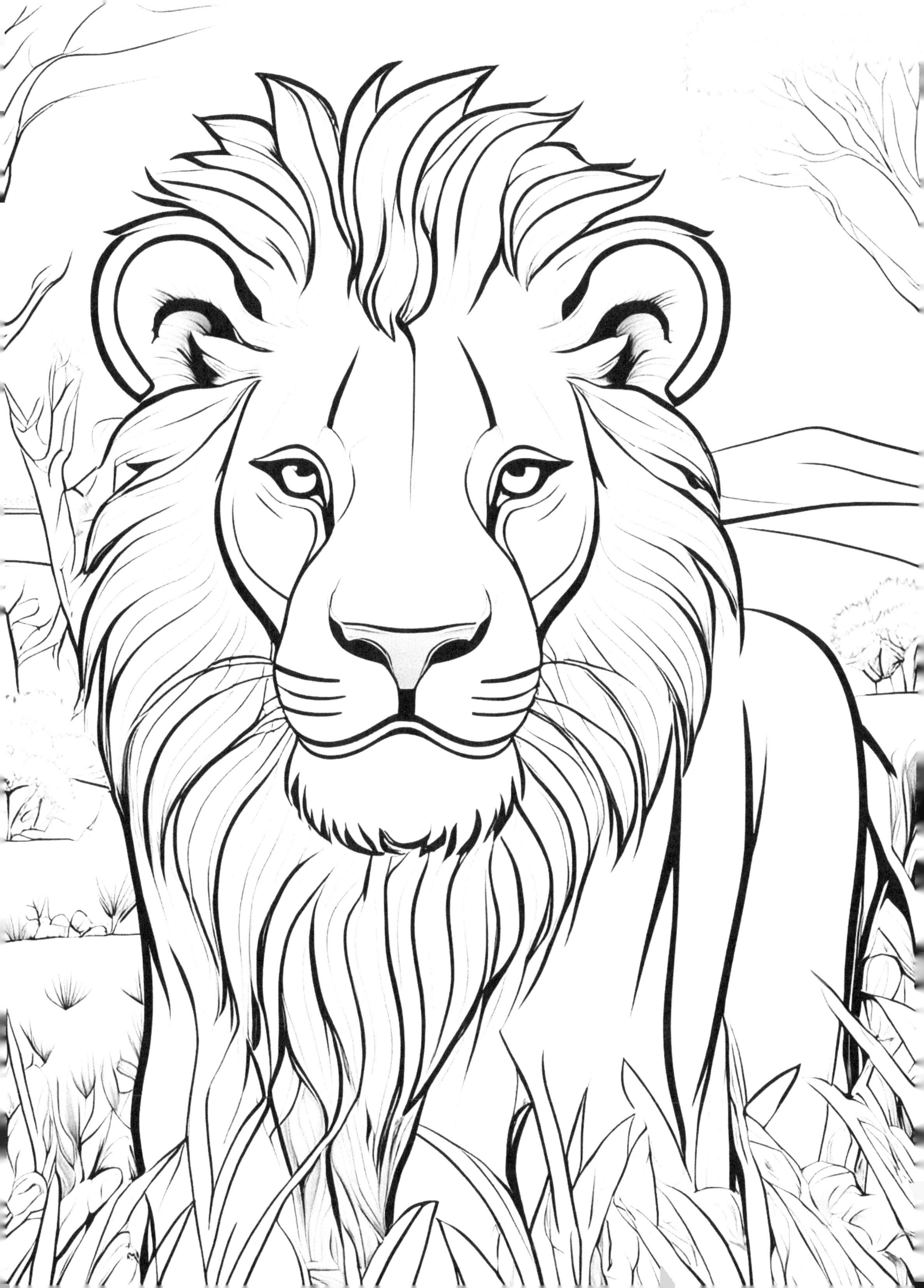

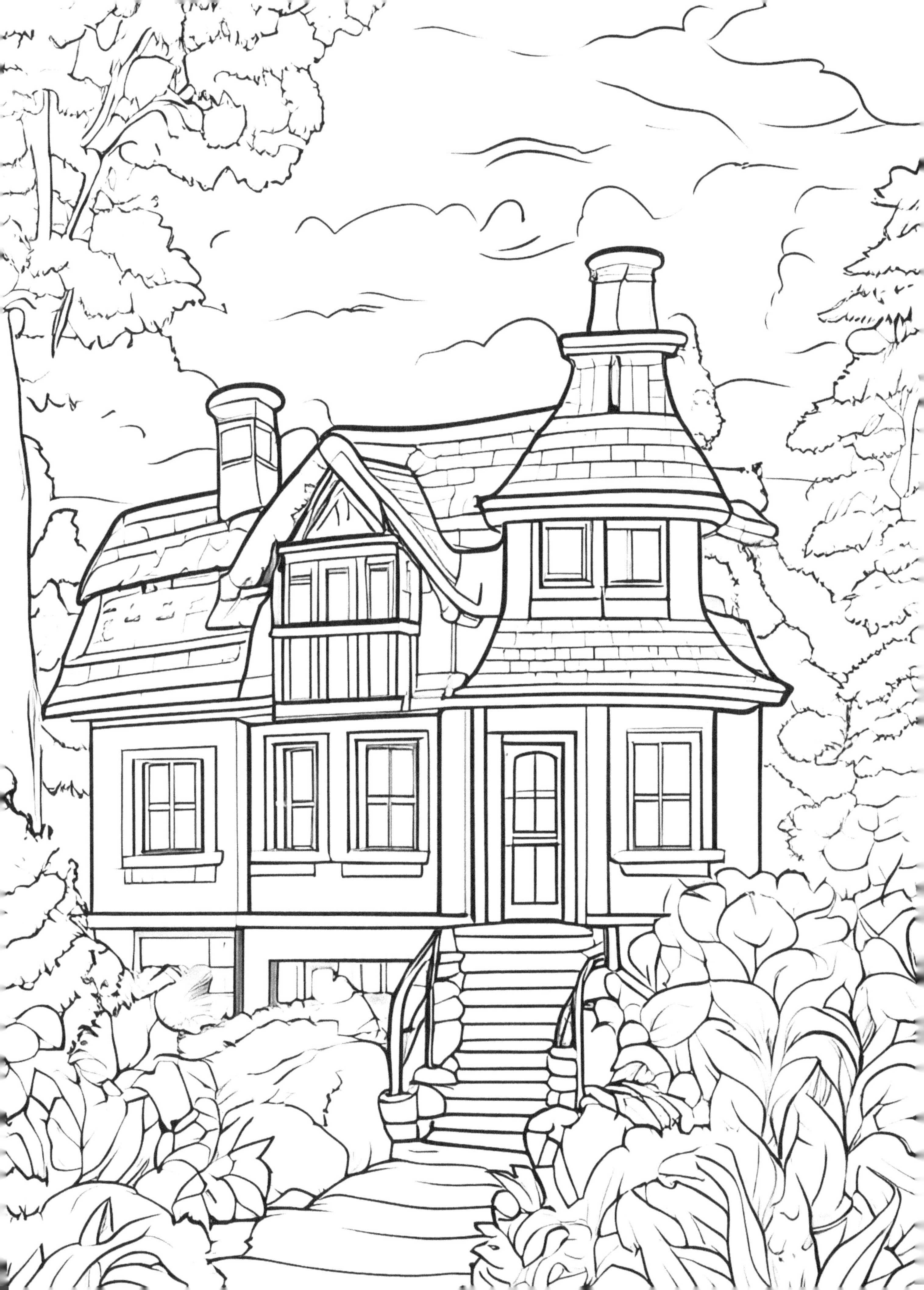

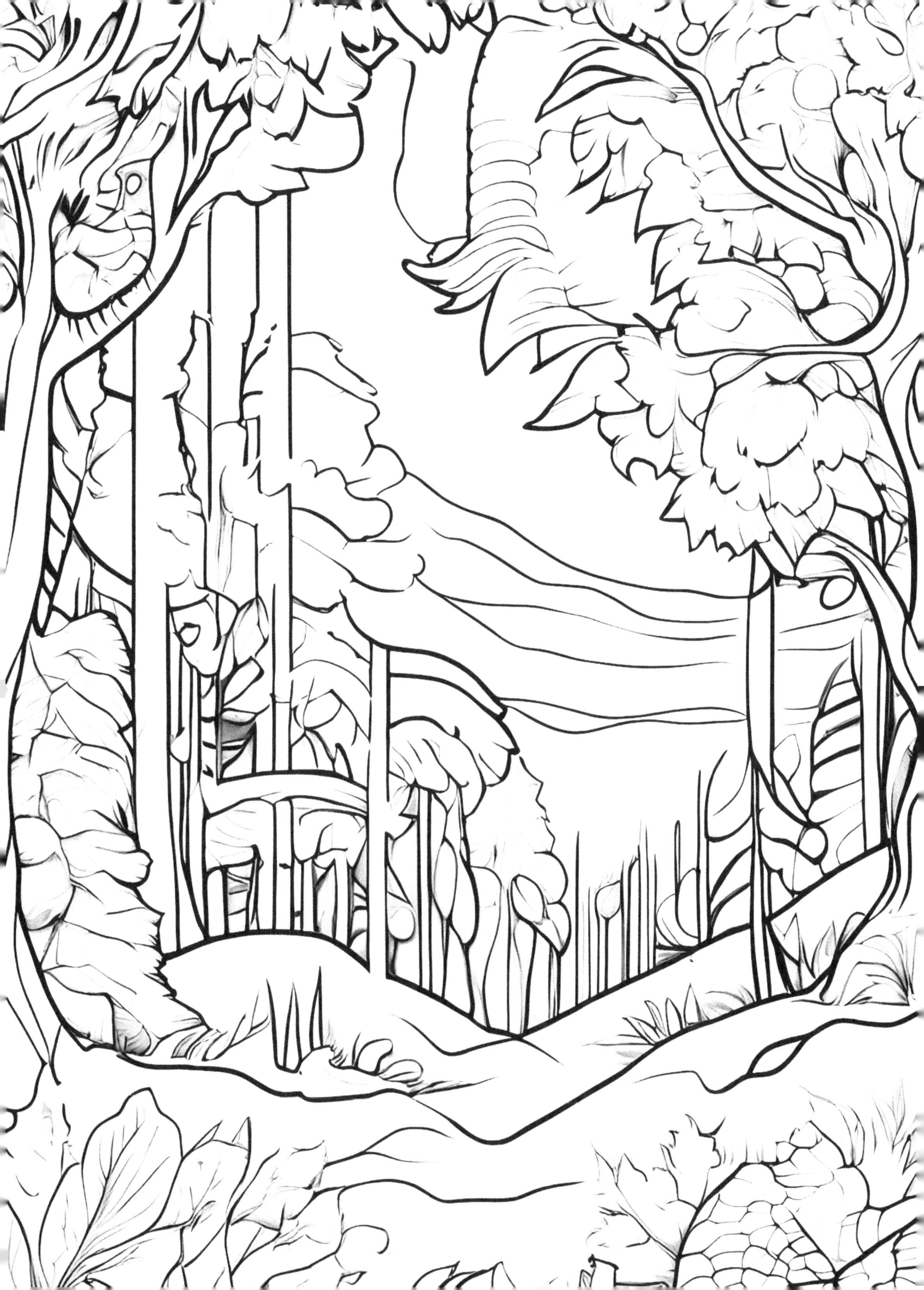

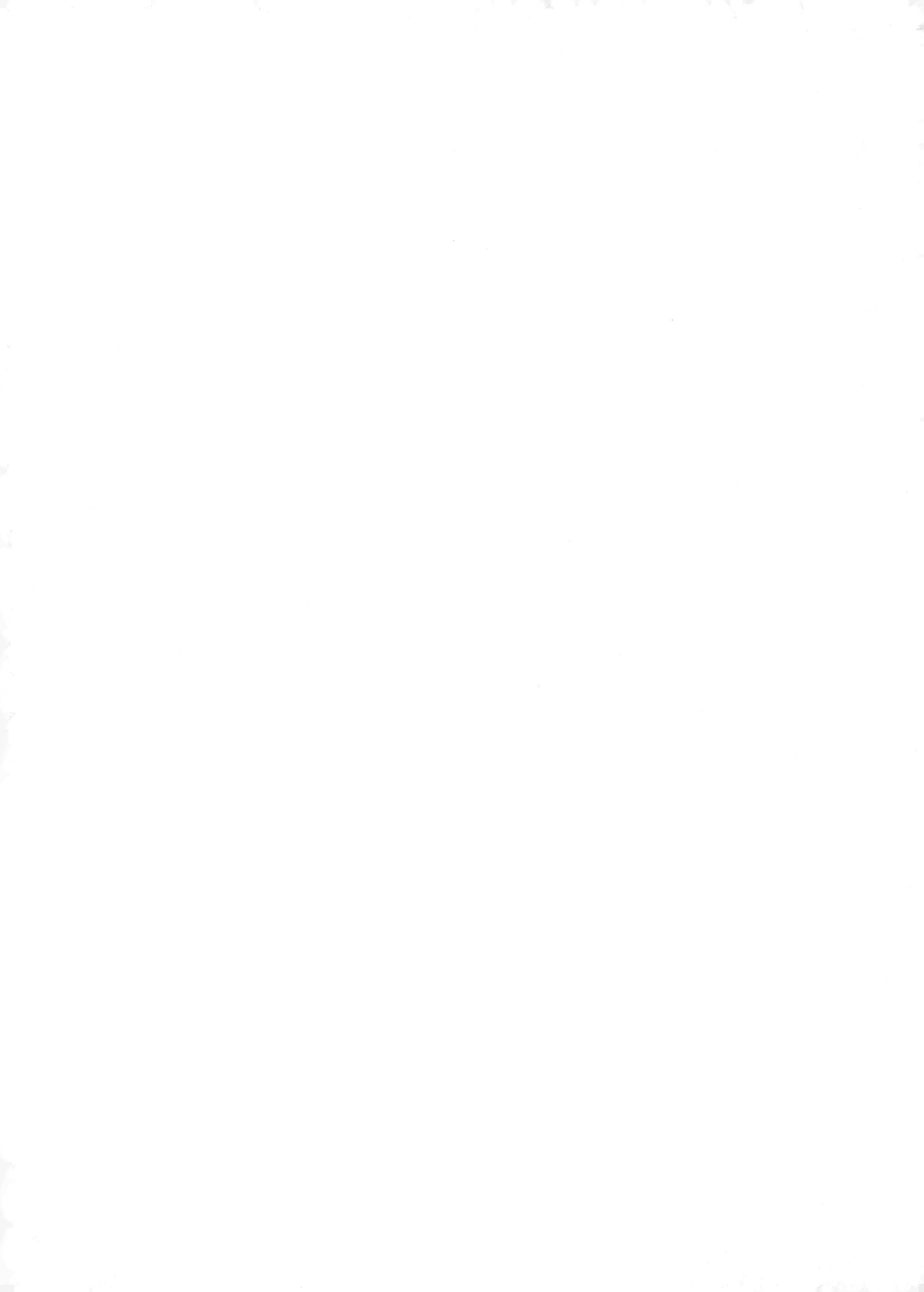

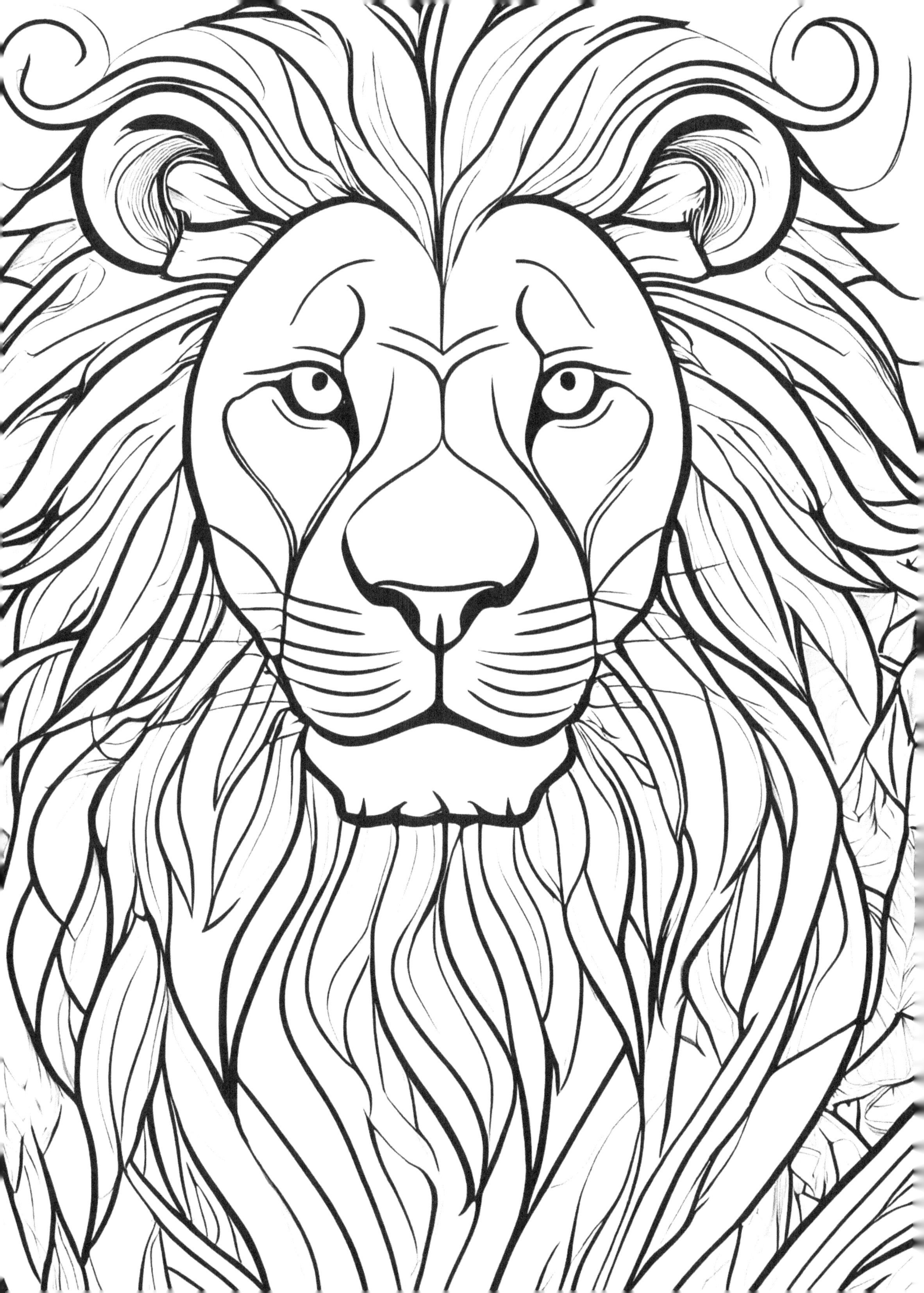

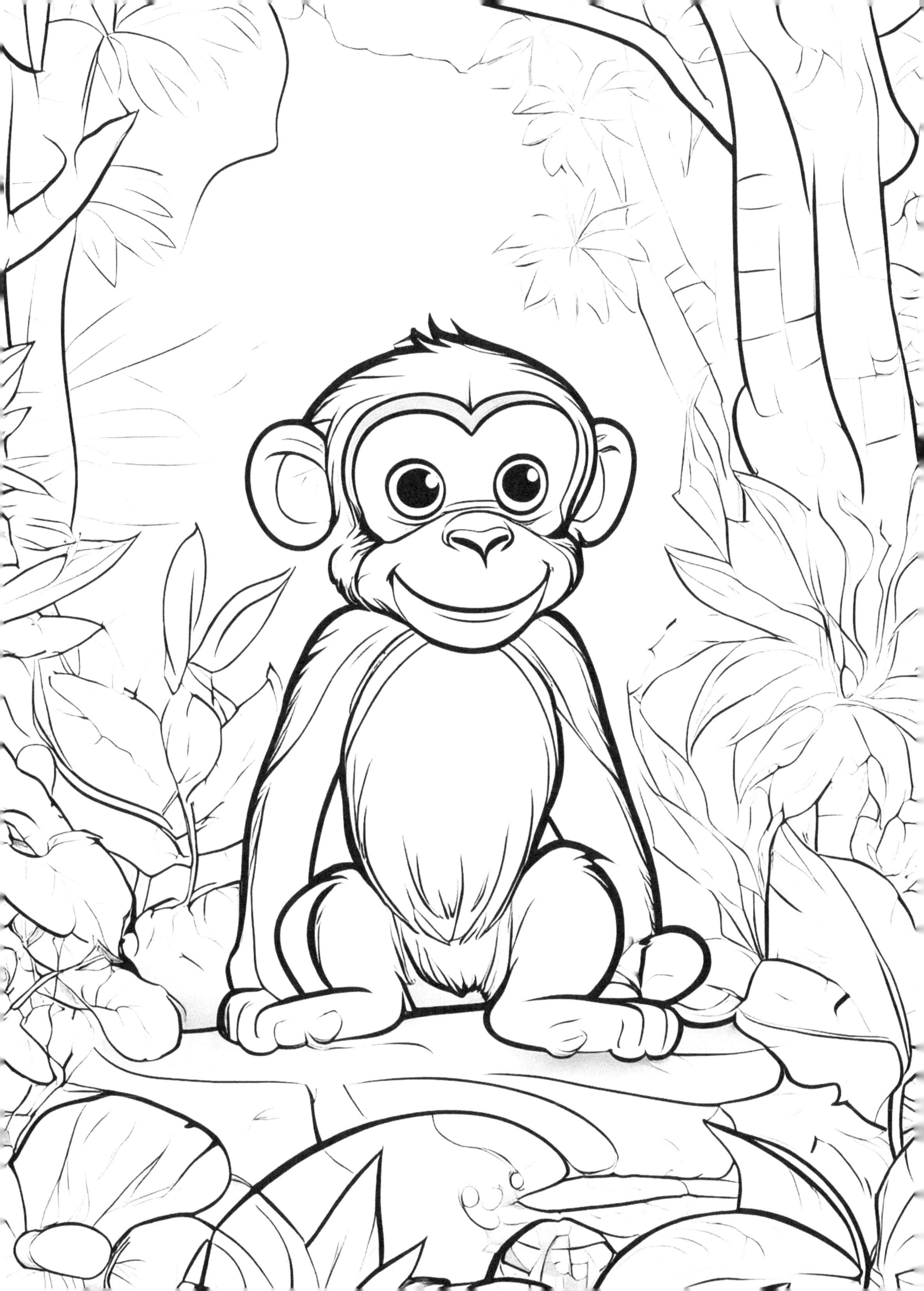

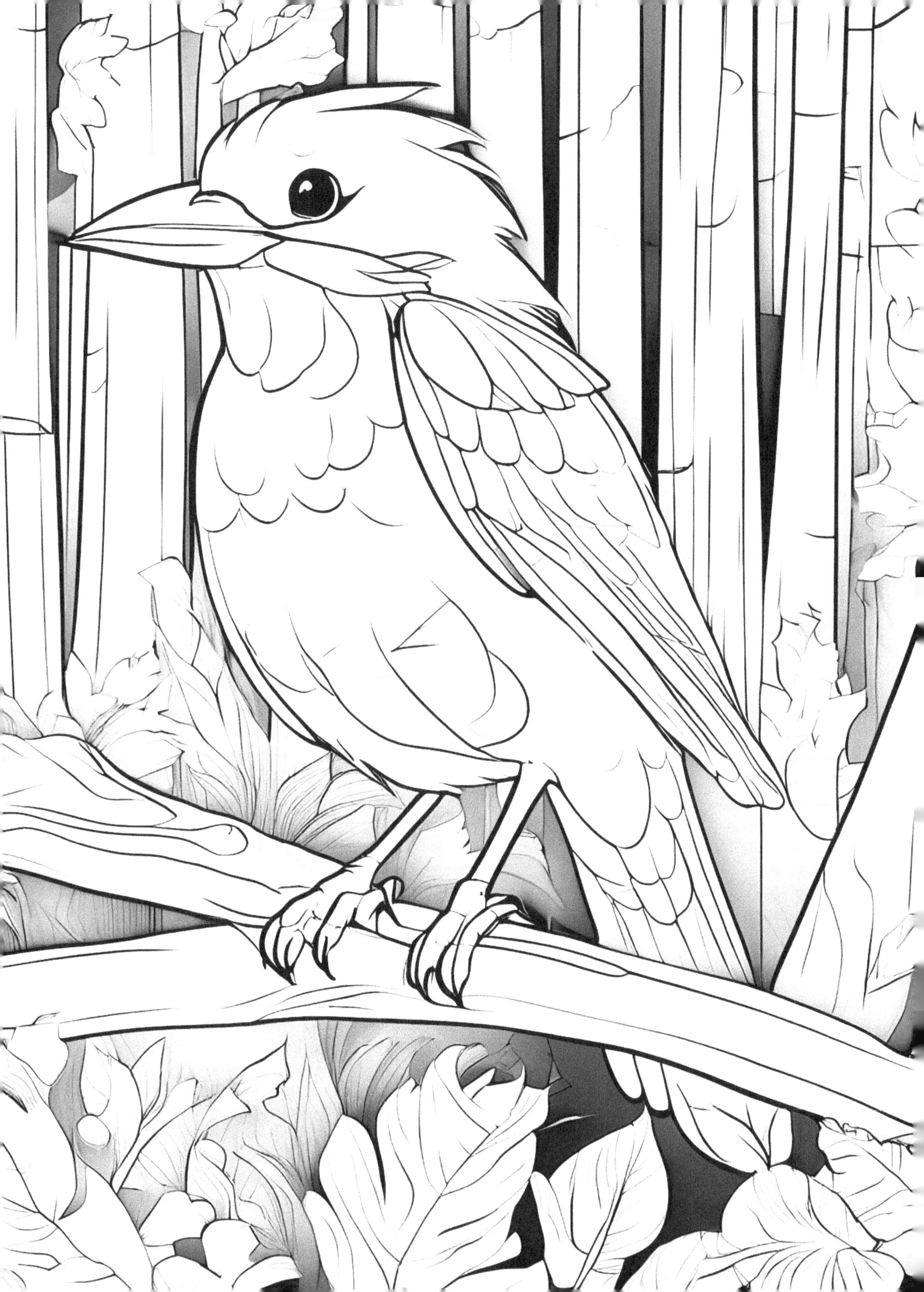

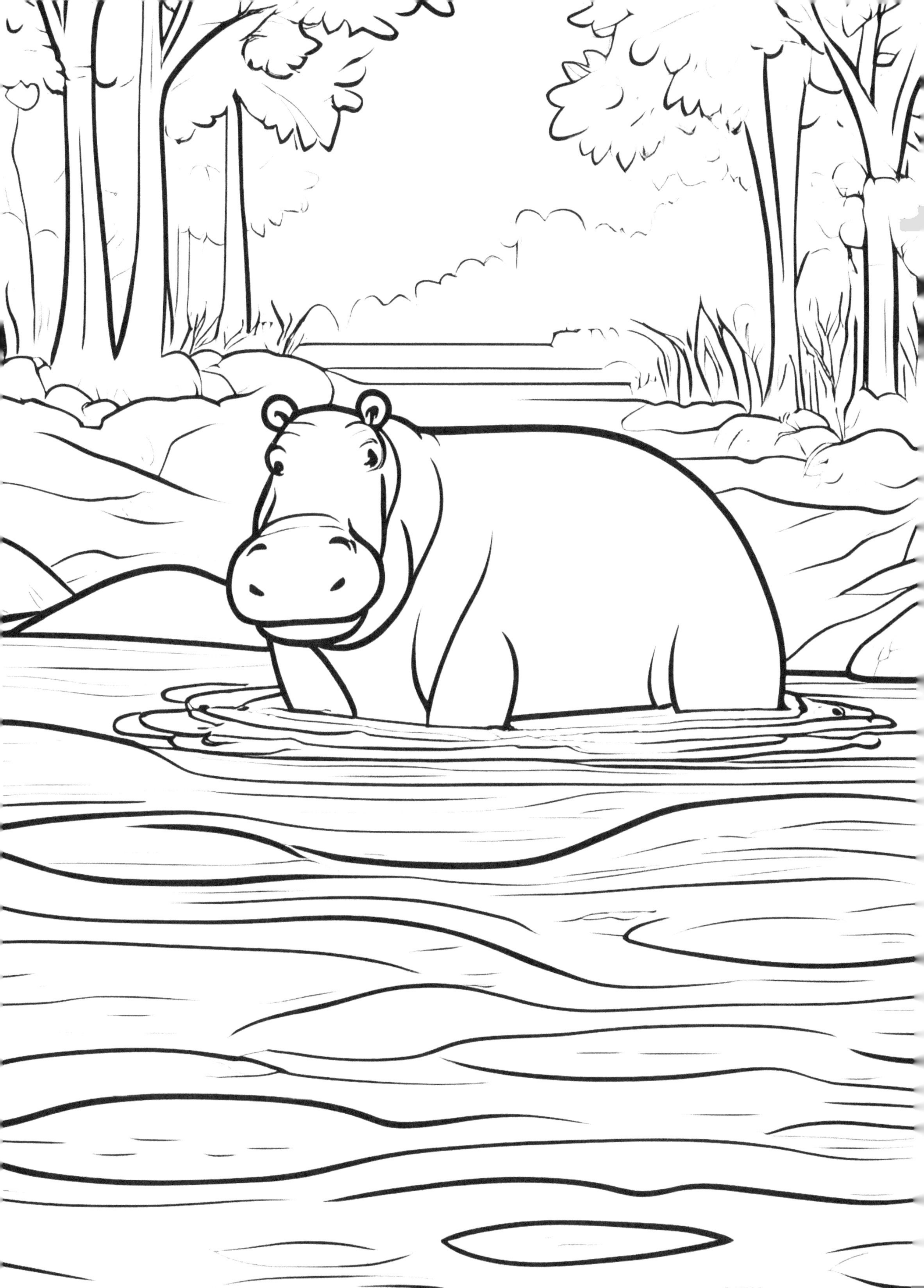

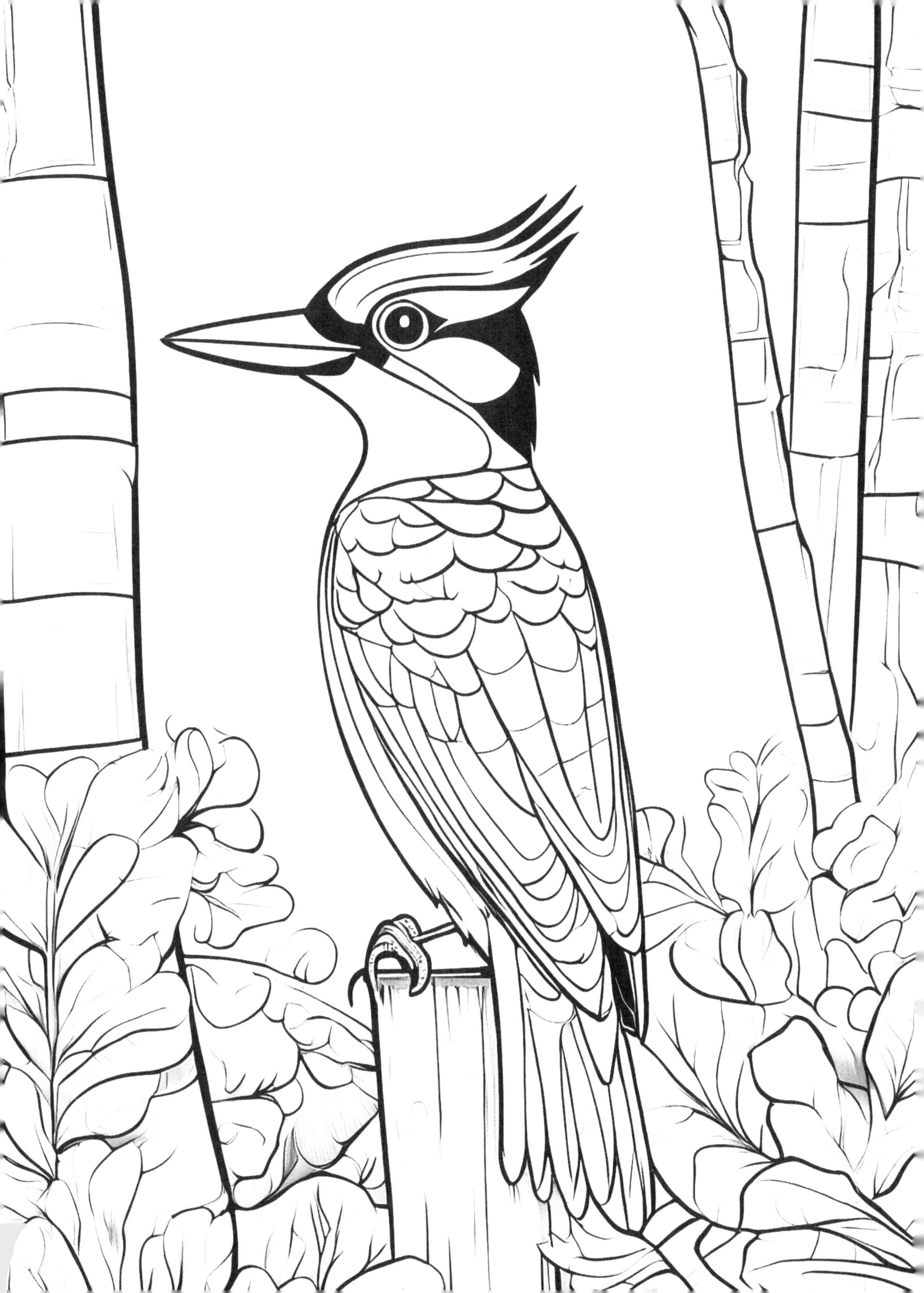

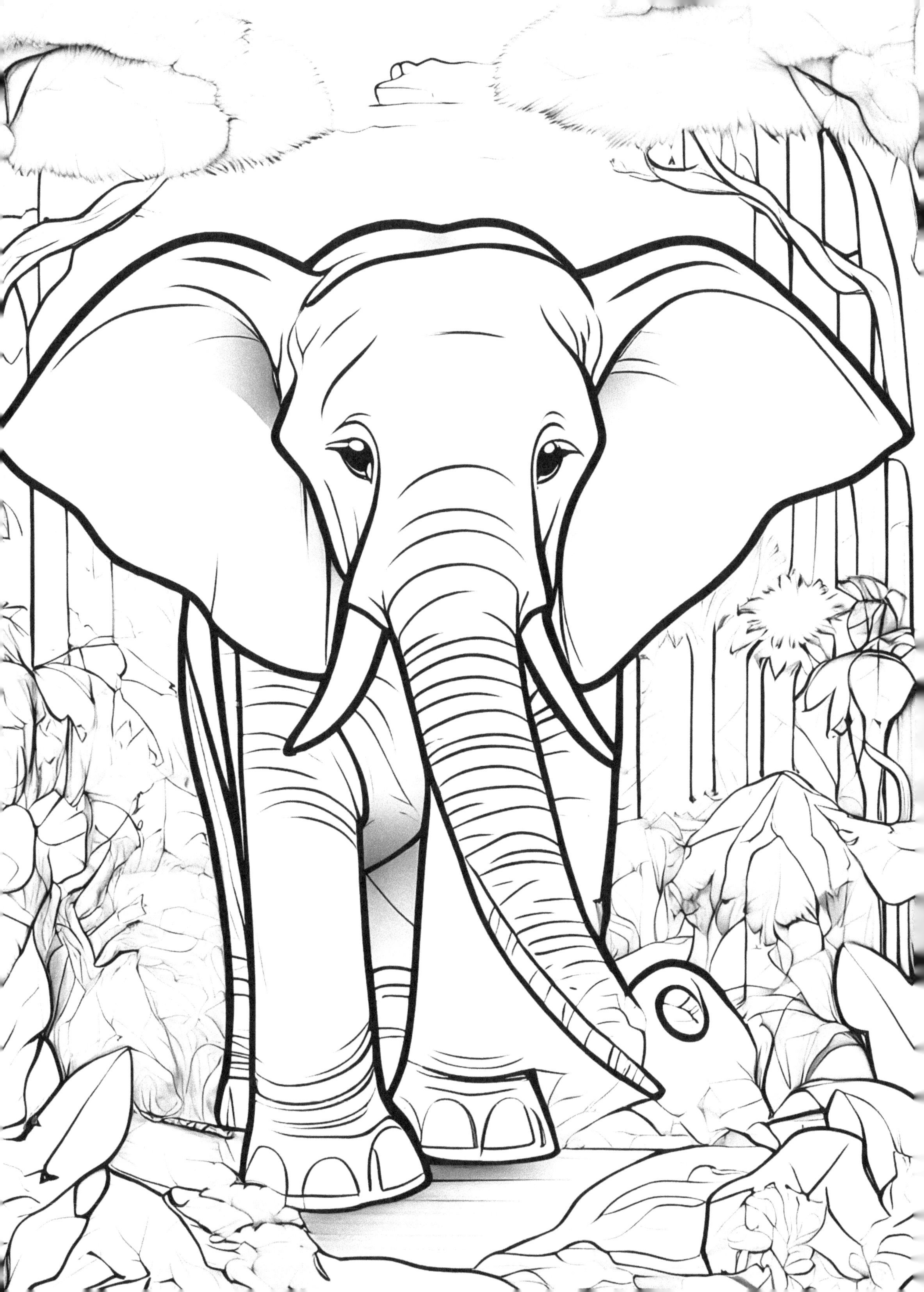

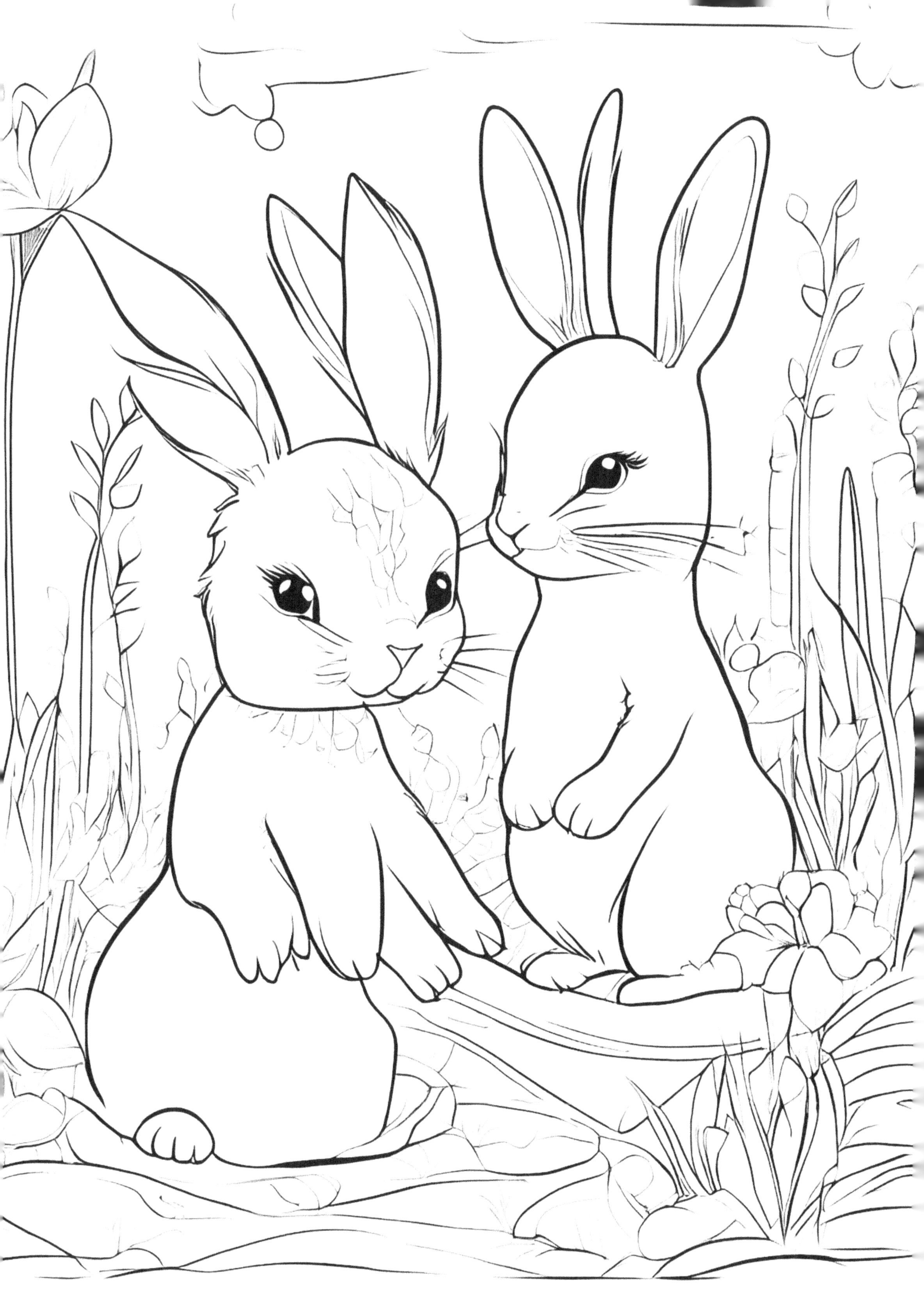